**Editor**
Mary S. Jones

**Managing Editor**
Ina Massler Levin, M.A.

**Cover Artist**
Brenda DiAntonis

**Art Manager**
Kevin Barnes

**Art Director**
CJae Froshay

**Imaging**
Rosa C. See

**Publisher**
Mary D. Smith, M.S. Ed.

**Author**

*Sarah Kartchner Clark, M.A.*

***Teacher Created Resources, Inc.***
6421 Industry Way
Westminster, CA 92683
www.teachercreated.com

**ISBN: 978-1-4206-3984-1**

*©2005 Teacher Created Resources, Inc.*
Reprinted, 2011
Made in U.S.A.

# Table of Contents

# Introduction

Today's children need opportunities to use their brains and to problem solve. The more children are exposed to problem solving now, the better prepared they will be for the future. Children need time to think about and explore answers. This book, *Mind Twisters*, is designed to challenge and stretch the brain. These brain teasers will get your students thinking about problems and how to arrive at solutions. This book is a compilation of fun, creative, unique, and challenging experiences for your students. It provides ways to exercise and develop brain power.

The mind twisters can be used to start off the day, or they can be used to enrich different areas of your curriculum. All of the mind twisters are designed to be completed by individual learners, although you may choose to pair your students with partners as needed.

*Mind Twisters* is divided into four sections. These sections are *Brain Stretchers, Mathematical Workouts, Problem Solving Puzzlers,* and *Critical Thinking Connections*. Some of the activities are meant for right–brain thinking while others are more for left–brain thinking. Each section focuses on a different part of the brain to provide a full brain workout.

## ✏ Brain Stretchers

The brain stretchers in this first section will enrich and increase the vocabulary of your students. These activities will develop such skills as creativity, complexity, analysis, originality, and elaboration. The use of words and language in these activities will also reinforce spelling, reading, and writing skills.

## ✏ Mathematical Workouts

Activities in this section will improve mathematical skills of your students while reviewing concepts you are already teaching. To complete the mathematical workouts, your students will develop such skills as collection, retention, recall, and use of information. In addition, they will further develop mathematical operations.

## ✏ Problem Solving Puzzlers

The problem solving puzzlers will challenge and push your students. The comfort zone will be redefined as students analyze and solve these puzzles. Your students will continue to develop skills such as risk-taking, trial and error, elaboration, and will require complex thinking skills.

## ✏ Critical Thinking Connections

It is important to develop different thinking domains, as each domain has a different aim and helps develop different skills. Critical thinking connections will provide your students with opportunities to examine, clarify, and evaluate an idea, belief, or action. Is it reasonable? Students need to infer, hypothesize, generalize, take a point of view, and find solutions. Activities in this section are open-ended and require critical thinking skills to complete. Encourage creativity and thorough investigation as students complete these activities.

# From Beginning to End

Can you turn the word "ADD" into "ZOO" in ten tries by changing one letter at a time?  Only use the clues if you really need to!

| A | D | D | |
|---|---|---|---|
| | | | help or assist |
| | | | a cover |
| | | | started a flame |
| | | | lice egg |
| | | | a seed from a tree |
| | | | a fish trap |
| | | | not old |
| | | | present time |
| | | | transport a car |
| | | | also |
| Z | O | O | |

**Extension**:

Can you create your own word puzzle?  Begin with a word and change it into a different one. Remember to create clues to give hints.

# Know Your ABCs

Put these words in alphabetical order.  Can you do it in just five minutes?

| | | |
|---|---|---|
| ancient | errand | backwards |
| emotions | axle | alliance |
| alligator | credible | eviction |
| ambulance | angrily | captain |
| acrobat | forcible | envy |

1. _____

2. _____

3. _____

4. _____

5. _____

6. _____

7. _____

8. _____

9. _____

10. _____

11. _____

12. _____

13. _____

14. _____

15. _____

# License Plate Limbo

Many license plates are personalized with a special message. Can you decode the following license plates? The first one has been done for you.

1. **IMHOT**

   I'm hot
   _____

2. **BURNRUBR**

   _____

3. **IGO4IT**

   _____

4. **YRPL8HR**

   _____

5. **BLKVELVT**

   _____

6. **LDYBG**

   _____

7. **LOVENU**

   _____

8. **RSECRET**

   _____

9. **AU2FAN**

   _____

10. **ANTQLVR**

    _____

11. **4NANGL**

    _____

12. **BBALSTR**

    _____

13. **PTCRUZR**

    _____

14. **IM2BZ**

    _____

15. **URNOZE**

    _____

16. **RESQ911**

    _____

*Brain Stretchers*

# Salt and Pepper

The words below commonly pair up with another word.  Write the missing half of each pair.

1. _____ and spice

2. _____ and blue

3. _____ and cents

4. _____ and proper

5. _____ and paper

6. _____ and fall

7. _____ and little

8. _____ and white

9. _____ and out

10. _____ and down

11. _____ and stones

12. _____ and thin

13. _____ and short

14. _____ and dogs

15. _____ and forth

16. _____ and quiet

17. _____ and sugar

18. _____ and nail

19. _____ and crackers

20. _____ and eggs

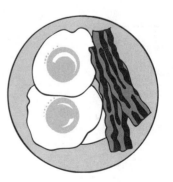

# What's in the Fridge?

Next to each letter of the alphabet, write at least one thing that starts with that letter that you might find in the refrigerator.  For example:  *A – apples, apricots, applesauce.*  How quickly can you come up with something for each letter?

A _____     N _____

B _____     O _____

C _____     P _____

D _____     Q _____

E _____     R _____

F _____     S _____

G _____     T _____

H _____     U _____

I _____     V _____

J _____     W _____

K _____     X _____

L _____     Y _____

M _____     Z _____

# What's a Palindrome?

A *palindrome* is a word, phrase, sentence, or number that can be read forwards or backwards. Write a palindrome that relates to each word or phrase below. An example has been done for you.

> another name for mother=mom

1. female sheep _____

2. short for Robert _____

3. a little child _____

4. twelve o'clock _____

5. amazing _____

6. a type of flower _____

7. first woman _____

8. to choke _____

9. noise of baby chick _____

10. keeps baby clean _____

11. on the screen _____

12. songs sung alone _____

13. distress, cry for help _____

14. father _____

15. soda _____

16. very fast car _____

17. a girl's name beginning with "H" _____

18. paper that says you own land _____

# Decode the Code

Different kinds of languages and codes help people who cannot see or hear well communicate. The Braille alphabet helps those who cannot see. The Sign Language Manual Alphabet helps those who cannot hear. Morse code has also been used as a language to help in many circumstances. Use the alphabet code below to decode the message at the bottom of the page.

| | | | | | |
|---|---|---|---|---|---|
| A | = | 26 | N | = | 13 |
| B | = | 25 | O | = | 12 |
| C | = | 24 | P | = | 11 |
| D | = | 23 | Q | = | 10 |
| E | = | 22 | R | = | 9 |
| F | = | 21 | S | = | 8 |
| G | = | 20 | T | = | 7 |
| H | = | 19 | U | = | 6 |
| I | = | 18 | V | = | 5 |
| J | = | 17 | W | = | 4 |
| K | = | 16 | X | = | 3 |
| L | = | 15 | Y | = | 2 |
| M | = | 14 | Z | = | 1 |

Decode this message:

| 18 | 14 | 26 | 20 | 18 | 13 | 22 |
|----|----|----|----|----|----|----|

| 2 | 12 | 6 | 9 | 8 | 22 | 15 | 21 |
|---|----|---|---|---|----|----|----|

| 8 | 6 | 24 | 24 | 22 | 22 | 23 | 18 | 13 | 20 | ! |
|---|---|----|----|----|----|----|----|----|----|---|

10

# That's an Oxymoron!

An *oxymoron* is two words that when put together, mean the opposite of each other.  They are contradictory.  Match the words in list A with the words in list B to create an oxymoron. Combine the words together on the lines below.  A sample has been done for you.

| List A | List B |
|--------|--------|
| ~~tight~~ | ~~slacks~~ |
| deafening | dead |
| healthy | difference |
| jumbo | force |
| living | live |
| mournful | optimist |
| peace | party |
| pretty | scream |
| same | shrimp |
| silent | silence |
| taped | tan |
| work | ugly |

1. _____tight_____        _____slacks_____

2. _____        _____

3. _____        _____

4. _____        _____

5. _____        _____

6. _____        _____

7. _____        _____

8. _____        _____

9. _____        _____

10. _____        _____

11. _____        _____

12. _____        _____

# Testing the Experiment

How many words of four or more letters can you make from the word *experimentation*? You may only use each letter as many times as it appears.

## E X P E R I M E N T A T I O N

Words with four letters:

Words with five letters:

Words with six letters:

Words with seven letters:

Words with eight or more letters:

# What's in Box #1?

Match the clues from page 14 to their **synonyms** below. Then, write the corresponding letter on the line above the clue. You will not use all of the letters. The five clues will help you figure out what's in the box.

| | | | | | | |
|---|---|---|---|---|---|---|
| A | = | huge | | N | = | nap |
| B | = | spoke | | O | = | pail |
| C | = | little | | P | = | big |
| D | = | rabbit | | Q | = | father |
| E | = | beautiful | | R | = | beach |
| F | = | yelled | | S | = | shut |
| G | = | choose | | T | = | gift |
| H | = | jumped | | U | = | pieces |
| I | = | fastest | | V | = | silent |
| J | = | skinny | | W | = | ill |
| K | = | allow | | X | = | giggle |
| L | = | wind | | Y | = | near |
| M | = | hunt | | Z | = | leave |

# What's in Box #1? *(cont.)*

See page 13 for directions.

**BOX #1**

**Clue 1:**

_____ _____ _____
pretty   pick   pick

**Clue 2:**

_____ _____ _____ _____
large  pretty  small  permit

**Clue 3:**

_____ _____ _____ _____ _____ _____ _____
close  small  seashore  enormous  present  small  hopped

**Clue 4:**

_____ _____ _____
breeze  enormous  close

**Clue 5:**

_____ _____ _____ _____ _____ _____ _____
shouted  pretty  enormous  present  hopped  pretty  seashore

What is in the box? _____

# What's in Box #2?

Match the clues from page 16 to their **antonyms** below. Then, write the corresponding letter on the line above the clue. You will not use all of the letters. The five clues will help you figure out what's in the box.

| | | | | | |
|---|---|---|---|---|---|
| A | = | sunny | N | = | first |
| B | = | dark | O | = | loud |
| C | = | day | P | = | many |
| D | = | good | Q | = | curved |
| E | = | open | R | = | sad |
| F | = | liquid | S | = | cold |
| G | = | in | T | = | lucky |
| H | = | over | U | = | up |
| I | = | dirty | V | = | happy |
| J | = | large | W | = | wet |
| K | = | mom | X | = | hard |
| L | = | love | Y | = | beautiful |
| M | = | empty | Z | = | late |

# What's in Box #2? *(cont.)*

See page 15 for directions.

**BOX #2**

**Clue 1:**

_____  _____  _____
happy  down  last

**Clue 2:**

_____  _____  _____  _____
dad  clean  night  dad

**Clue 3:**

_____  _____  _____  _____  _____  _____  _____
solid  quiet  happy  dry  cloudy  happy  bad

**Clue 4:**

_____  _____  _____  _____  _____
solid  clean  close  hate  bad

**Clue 5:**

_____  _____  _____  _____  _____  _____
out  quiet  cloudy  hate  clean  close

What is in the box? _____

# The Letter *E*

Use the clues to fill in the blanks in the following words.  All the words begin and end with the letter *e*.

1. e __ __ __ __ __ e                    to carry out

2. e __ __ __ e                          the national bird

3. e __ __ __ __ e                       to breathe out

4. e __ __ __ __ __ __ e                 used to send a letter

5. e __ __ __ __ e                       to get away

6. e __ __ __ __ __ __ __ e              to instill confidence

7. e __ __ __ __ __ __ e                 to make a guess

8. e __ __ __ __ e                       to tempt

9. e __ e                                a female sheep

10. e __ __ __ __ __ __ e                to clear out

Now try to fill in these blanks with words that begin with the letter *a* and end with the letter *e*.

11. a __ __ e                            capable

12. a __ __ __ __ __ __ e                jet

13. a __ e                              monkey

14. a __ __ __ e                        acute, obtuse

15. a __ __ __ __ __ __ e               rising higher

16. a __ __ __ e                        red fruit

17. a __ __ __ e                        treat poorly

18. a __ __ __ __ __ e                  very old

# Which Is the Imposter?

In each list below, circle the item that does not belong in the group and explain why on the line provided.

1. Gala, McIntosh, Bartlett, Red Delicious, Granny Smith, Jonathan

   _____

2. girl, niece, mom, sister, daughter-in-law, nephew, grandmother

   _____

3. February, March, November, October, December, August

   _____

4. cirrus, calculus, cumulus, stratus, cirrostratus, altocumulus

   _____

5. hexagon, octagon, oxygen, square, sphere, triangle, cube

   _____

6. centimeter, decimeter, kilometer, hectogram, kilogram, ounce, deciliter

   _____

7. red, yellow, blue, orange

   _____

8. factor, product, multiple, sum, multiply

   _____

9. dogwood, iris, rose, carnation, lily, tulip, orchid

   _____

10. rabbit, frog, toad, bunny, turtle, grasshopper, cricket

# Question of the Day

Write a question for each of the following answers.

1. **Question:**_____

   Answer:  An earthquake.

2. **Question:**_____

   Answer:  The giraffe and the zebra.

3. **Question:**_____

   Answer:  $1,349.90.

4. **Question:**_____

   Answer:  July 4, 1776.

5. **Question:**_____

   Answer:  Apricots, apples, and apes.

6. **Question:**_____

   Answer:  A marathon.

7. **Question:**_____

   Answer:  The *Mona Lisa*.

8. **Question:**_____

   Answer:  The *Nutcracker*.

9. **Question:**_____

   Answer:  Mark Twain.

10. **Question:**_____

    Answer:  Langston Hughes.

11. **Question:**_____

    Answer:  Every fourth Wednesday.

# The Long and Short of It

The following words (some are slang) are written in short form. Write the long form for each of these words in the blanks on the right. In the blanks at the bottom (#13–17), write both the short and long forms of five more words.

| | Short Form | Long Form |
|---|---|---|
| 1. | math | _____ |
| 2. | P.E. | _____ |
| 3. | ref | _____ |
| 4. | champ | _____ |
| 5. | TV | _____ |
| 6. | limo | _____ |
| 7. | doc | _____ |
| 8. | exam | _____ |
| 9. | phone | _____ |
| 10. | fridge | _____ |
| 11. | plane | _____ |
| 12. | prez | _____ |
| 13. | _____ | _____ |
| 14. | _____ | _____ |
| 15. | _____ | _____ |
| 16. | _____ | _____ |
| 17. | _____ | _____ |

# You're a Funny Bunny

Find an adjective that rhymes with a noun so that together, the two words have about the same meaning as the phrase given.  An example has been done for you.

1. unusual grizzly          _rare bear_____

2. feline pad              _____

3. equestrian class        _____

4. burned bread            _____

5. purple gorilla          _____

6. beetle embrace          _____

7. kind grizzly            _____

8. dog kiss                _____

9. loafing flower          _____

10. large swine            _____

11. crude man              _____

12. overweight kitty       _____

13. unhappy boy            _____

14. sunbathing adorer      _____

15. depressed father       _____

16. beetle carpet          _____

17. calm man               _____

18. skinny horse           _____

19. rodent home            _____

20. smooth hen             _____

# Cut It Short

Write the meaning of each abbreviation or acronym.

1. ASAP _____

2. Etc. _____

3. NYC _____

4. USA _____

5. NASA _____

6. NBA _____

7. D.A. _____

8. I.O.U. _____

9. RR _____

10. Dr. _____

11. FBI _____

12. IRS _____

13. B.C. _____

14. D.A.R.E. _____

15. C.O.D. _____

16. NFL _____

17. P.S. _____

18. VT _____

19. Apr. _____

20. EMT _____

# Word Chains

Fill in all the blanks with a 3-, 4-, 5-, or 6-letter word, depending on the number of blanks given.  Each word must begin with the last letter of the preceding word. The first word may start with any letter. You may use each word only once.  (Race with another student if you are up for a challenge.)

1. ＿＿ ＿＿ ＿＿

2. ＿＿ ＿＿ ＿＿ ＿＿ ＿＿

3. ＿＿ ＿＿ ＿＿ ＿＿ ＿＿ ＿＿

4. ＿＿ ＿＿ ＿＿ ＿＿ ＿＿

5. ＿＿ ＿＿ ＿＿ ＿＿

6. ＿＿ ＿＿ ＿＿

7. ＿＿ ＿＿ ＿＿ ＿＿ ＿＿ ＿＿

8. ＿＿ ＿＿ ＿＿ ＿＿

9. ＿＿ ＿＿ ＿＿ ＿＿

10. ＿＿ ＿＿ ＿＿ ＿＿ ＿＿

11. ＿＿ ＿＿ ＿＿ ＿＿ ＿＿ ＿＿

12. ＿＿ ＿＿ ＿＿

13. ＿＿ ＿＿ ＿＿

14. ＿＿ ＿＿ ＿＿ ＿＿ ＿＿ ＿＿

15. ＿＿ ＿＿ ＿＿ ＿＿

16. ＿＿ ＿＿ ＿＿ ＿＿ ＿＿

17. ＿＿ ＿＿ ＿＿ ＿＿ ＿＿ ＿＿

18. ＿＿ ＿＿ ＿＿

19. ＿＿ ＿＿ ＿＿ ＿＿ ＿＿

20. ＿＿ ＿＿ ＿＿ ＿＿

# Super Solutions

Can you find the answers to these word problems? Be sure to explain your answers, if needed.

| | |
|---|---|
| 1. What is the mode (most frequently appearing item) of this data?<br><br>24, 26, 28, 30, 30, 31, 34, 37, 39 | 2. Irene was traveling on an airplane with her family. The plane left the airport at 10:15 A.M. She was served breakfast 42 minutes into the flight. If she took 13 minutes to eat her breakfast, at what time did Irene finish eating? |
| 3. Jason was in a pie-eating contest. He was able to eat 3 cream pies that each contained 15 cherries. How many cherries did Jason eat in all? | 4. John wants to buy a new video game and has saved up $12.50. If the video game costs $14.95, how much more does he need to save in order to buy the video game? |
| 5. Frank and Ann have birthdays that are 15 days apart. Frank's birthday is on April 21st, and Ann's birthday is after his. When is Ann's birthday? | 6. Cynthia was swimming laps in the pool one morning. She did 15 laps of freestyle, 12 laps of butterfly, and 10 laps of breaststroke. How many laps did Cynthia swim in all? |

     24     

# Athletically Inclined

Do you participate on a sports team?  The six children in this chart each compete in a different sport.  From the clues below, determine the sport that each child plays.  Mark the correct boxes with a "Y" for *Yes* and the incorrect boxes with a "N" for *No*.

| | Soccer | Basketball | Volleyball | Baseball | Swimming | Track |
|---|---|---|---|---|---|---|
| **Anne** | | | | | | |
| **Elise** | | | | | | |
| **Ethan** | | | | | | |
| **Katie** | | | | | | |
| **Logan** | | | | | | |
| **Kevin** | | | | | | |

**Clues:**

1. Ethan needs water to compete.

2. Anne's sport requires kneepads.

3. Elise dribbles a ball with her hands.

4. Katie's sport begins and ends with the same letters as Elise's sport.

5. Logan is a goalie.

6. Kevin runs in circles.

# Money Matters

Find your way through this money maze. Some of the money amounts do not add up. Find the path of **correct money amounts** beginning at *Start* and ending at *Finish*. Connect **all** the boxes of correct money amounts together using arrows. You may go up, down, sideways, or diagonally. The first arrow has been placed for you.

| | | | |
|---|---|---|---|
| **$ FINISH $** | 6 nickels<br>+ 4 dimes<br>80 cents | **$ START $** | 6 pennies<br>6 dimes<br>+ 1 quarter<br>$1.01 |
| 5 dimes<br>+ 5 quarters<br>$1.25 | 11 quarters<br>= $2.75 | 3 pennies<br>3 nickels<br>+ 3 dimes<br>58 cents | 8 nickels<br>+ 3 quarters<br>$1.15 |
| 7 pennies<br>6 dimes<br>+ 1 quarter<br>92 cents | 12 quarters<br>= $3.25 | 7 nickels<br>+ 7 dimes<br>$1.05 | 10 dimes<br>+ 1 nickel<br>15 cents |
| 24 pennies<br>+ 1 quarter<br>49 cents | 4 pennies<br>+ 3 nickels<br>19 cents | 14 pennies<br>+ 6 dimes<br>64 cents | 1 nickel<br>1 dime<br>+ 1 quarter<br>44 cents |
| 5 pennies<br>2 dimes<br>+ 2 quarter<br>75 cents | 8 nickels<br>= 50 cents | 4 pennies<br>+ 7 nickels<br>39 cents | 11 pennies<br>+ 7 dimes<br>78 cents |
| 2 pennies<br>+ 3 quarters<br>76 cents | 8 pennies<br>+ 6 dimes<br>68 cents | 2 nickels<br>+ 4 dimes<br>48 cents | 19 nickels<br>= 95 cents |
| 11 pennies<br>+ 5 nickels<br>41 cents | 7 pennies<br>+ 5 nickels<br>35 cents | 2 pennies<br>6 nickels<br>+ 7 dimes<br>$1.02 | 3 nickels<br>3 dimes<br>+ 3 quarters<br>$1.20 |

26

# Sequencing Squares

Start with *Figure A* and divide it into fourths, the result is *Figure B*. *Figure C* shows this division done one more time, dividing each square into fourths again.

| **Figure A** | **Figure B** | **Figure C** |

If you did this two more times, how many squares would you have? _____

Explain your answer. _____

_____

_____

_____

_____

_____

_____

_____

_____

# Question Quiz

In each box below there is an answer to a mathematical word problem. Write a mathematical word problem for each answer. Be sure to show how you can solve the math problem. A sample has been done for you.

---

**Answer: There are 20 animals missing from the zoo.**

Question: The Willow Park Zoo holds exactly 100 animals. When the zookeeper walked through the whole zoo, he counted only 80 animals. How many animals are missing from the zoo?

$$100 - 80 = 20$$

---

**Answer: There are 24 butterflies all together.**

Question: _____

_____

_____

_____

---

**Answer: There are six students in each group.**

Question: _____

_____

_____

_____

---

**Answer: Each child receives one free pass.**

Question: _____

_____

_____

_____

---

# My Favorite Day

If you got to pick how you spent every minute of your day, what would you do? How much time would you spend doing these things? Use the circle below to create a pie graph of how you would spend your free day. A pie graph is one whole part divided into smaller parts. Add approximate percentages to each part when you are finished. Then, write five questions on the lines below that can be answered using your pie graph.

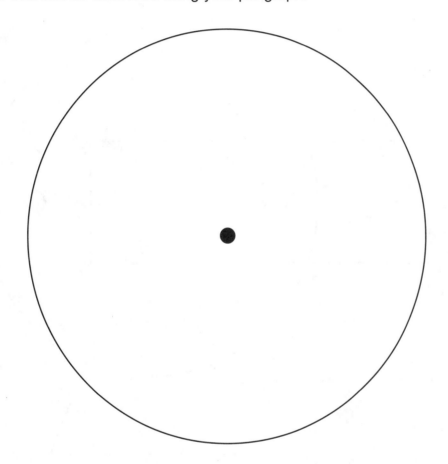

Create your own questions.

1. _____

2. _____

3. _____

4. _____

5. _____

# Geometrically Speaking

Are you ready for a geometrical challenge?  Each section of the figure below is labeled with a letter.  Your task is to find out which whole number goes in each section and what color it should be.  Use the following clues to help you solve this problem.  You may want to color/label all of the given information first.  Write your answers in the appropriate sections.

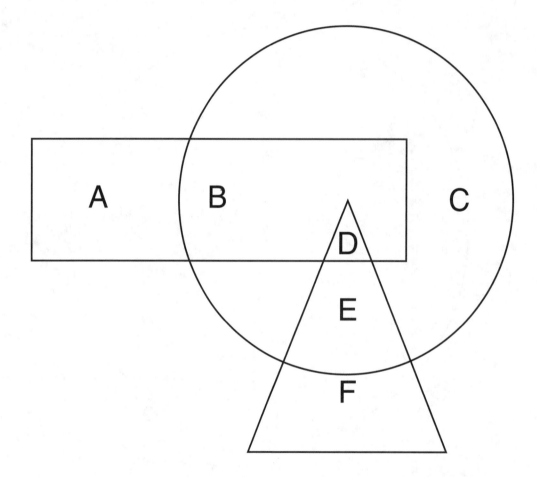

## Clues

1. The sum of the triangle is 15.

2. The section that is in all three shapes is colored green.

3. The rectangle has the red, white, and green sections in it.

4. The orange section is the number 8.

5. The product of section D and the blue section is 21.

6. The 5 section is purple.

7. A is red.

8. The sum of the rectangle is 11.

9. E is blue.

10. The sum of the circle is 20.

11. The sum of A and B is 8.

30

# Calots and Wiggles

1. These figures are *calots*:

2. None of these are *calots*:

  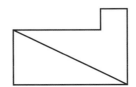 

3. What makes something a *calot*? According to your definition, draw three other figures that are *calots*.

4. These figures are *wiggles*:

5. None of these are *wiggles*:

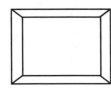  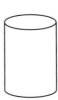

6. What makes something a *wiggle*? According to your definition, draw three other figures that are *wiggles*.

# Is It Symmetrical?

How many lines of symmetry does each figure have?

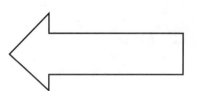

1. _____

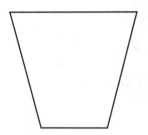

4. _____

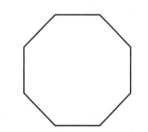

2. _____

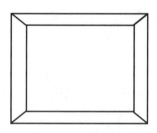

5. _____

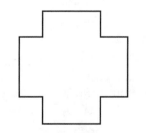

3. _____

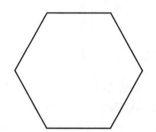

6. _____

# Number Sentences

How many number sentences can you make using combinations of these numbers? You can only use each number once, and you must use all of the numbers. You may use any combination of the number operations (addition, subtraction, multiplication, and division) to create your number sentences. Remember to solve each number sentence. (Note: Make sure the answer to your number sentence is a positive, whole number.)

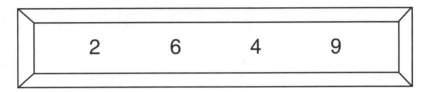

Examples:

$(2 + 6 - 4) \times 9 = 36$

$4 \times 6 \div 2 + 9 = 21$

_____

_____

_____

_____

_____

_____

_____

_____

_____

# Reckless Rearranging

Look at the group of numbers in the box below. Rearrange them in the circles below so that five sets of three numbers each add up to 20. One group has been done for you. (Those numbers cannot be used again.)

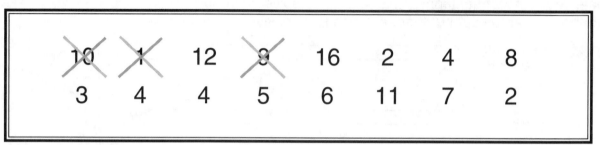

Guidelines to remember:

- Each group can only have these numbers.

- You can only use each number as many times as it appears.

- The sum must equal 20.

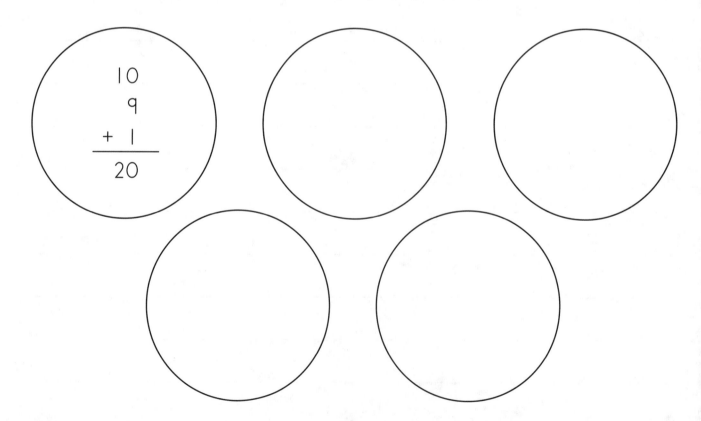

There is one number left over. Which number is it? _____

# Tricky Shapes

Look at the figure below. How many triangles are there? (Hint: Don't forget to look for the upside down triangles, or the ones you can make by combining triangles.)

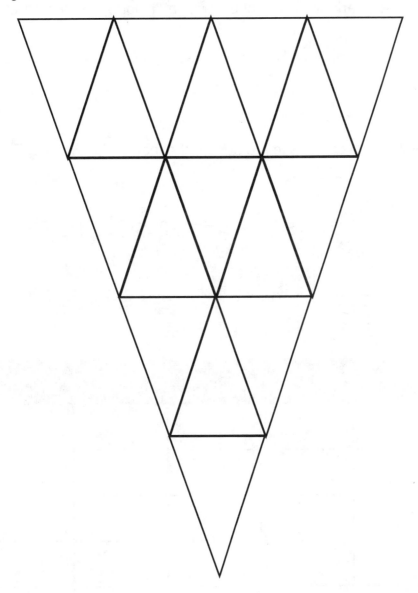

How many quadrilaterals are in the figure below?

# Final Grades

Mrs. Smith was grading the math tests as each of her six students awaited the results. Some of the students had studied and some had not. Using the clues below, determine each child's grade on the math test. Mark each correct box with a "Y" for *Yes* and each incorrect box with an "N" for *No*.

1. Paige, who did not get an *A* on her test, scored higher than Dwayne and Tanner.

2. Peyton and Tanner both scored higher than Eve.

3. Dwayne received a C on his test.

4. No two students received the same grade on the test.

5. Andrew scored 100% on his test.

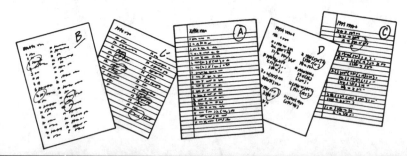

|  | A+ | A | B | C | C– | D |
|---|---|---|---|---|---|---|
| **Paige** |  |  |  |  |  |  |
| **Peyton** |  |  |  |  |  |  |
| **Tanner** |  |  |  |  |  |  |
| **Andrew** |  |  |  |  |  |  |
| **Eve** |  |  |  |  |  |  |
| **Dwayne** |  |  |  |  |  |  |

**Extension:**

Do you think most of the students in this group studied for this test? Why or why not? Explain your reasoning.

# What Comes Next?

The number sentences in each exercise follow a pattern.  Find the pattern, continue it for two more lines, and then check your answer on a calculator.

| | | |
|---|---|---|
| 64 x 1 = 64 | 24 x 4 = 96 | 6 x 7 + 8 = 50 |
| 64 x 2 = 128 | 24 x 44 = 1,056 | 65 x 7 + 7 = 462 |
| 64 x 3 = 192 | 24 x 444 = 10,656 | 654 x 7 + 6 = 4,584 |

_____    _____    _____

_____    _____    _____

Now make up some number sentences of your own that follow a pattern.  Be sure to solve each number sentence.  You can use a calculator if needed.

| Pattern #1 | Pattern #2 | Pattern #3 |
|---|---|---|

_____    _____    _____

_____    _____    _____

_____    _____    _____

_____    _____    _____

_____    _____    _____

## Extension:

Exchange your paper with another student.  See if he or she can discover your patterns.

# Figure It Out!

Andy, Bob, and Allison each have a different last name and a different pet. Use the grid and the list of clues below to determine who has what pet and what is each child's full name. Mark each correct box with a "Y" for *Yes* and mark each incorrect box with a "N" for *No*.

1. The Smiths' daughter has a cat.

2. Andy is short for Andrea.

3. No letters from a child's first name appear in the child's last name.

4. The Kings' son has a pet rabbit.

5. The Furths' child has a pet snake.

|  | First Name | | | Type of Pet | | |
|---|---|---|---|---|---|---|
|  | **Andy** | **Bob** | **Allison** | **cat** | **rabbit** | **snake** |
| **Smith** |  |  |  |  |  |  |
| **King** |  |  |  |  |  |  |
| **Furth** |  |  |  |  |  |  |

(Last Name)

Now create your own problem that can be solved using the grid below. Write clear and concise clues and be sure to double check them for accuracy. Solve the puzzle first and then share it with a friend.

|  |  |  |  |  |  |  |
|---|---|---|---|---|---|---|
|  |  |  |  |  |  |  |
|  |  |  |  |  |  |  |
|  |  |  |  |  |  |  |
|  |  |  |  |  |  |  |

# Solve the Puzzle

Are you ready for a puzzle? Use the figure below and the following clues to solve this problem. Notice that each section of the figure is labeled with a letter. Find out what number goes in each section and what color it should be. Be sure to double check your work.

**Clues:**

1. The number in the red section is twice as much as the number in the F section.

2. The yellow section is five.

3. The smallest number is in the blue section.

4. The sum of the numbers in E and G is thirteen.

5. The only prime number is in E.

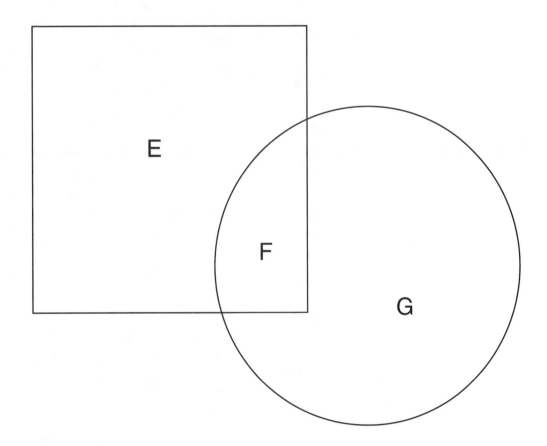

Explain the strategies you used to solve this puzzle._____

_____

_____

# Triangulation

The figure below is a sample of the concept of triangular numbers. There are 15 circles in the shape of a triangle. Can you think of more triangular numbers? The smallest triangular number is 3. Draw four other examples of triangular numbers below. You may begin with 3.

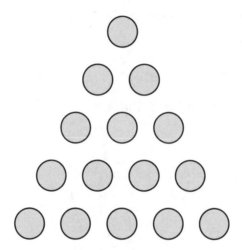

---

# Stars and Stripes

Fill in the missing spaces on the grid below.

Explain the rules of the grid: _____

_____

_____

Now, try it again with this grid:

Explain the rules of the grid: _____

_____

# Keep the Change

List the coins you would give each person below to make change for his or her dollar.

1. Damon wants 15 coins for his dollar. _____

2. Haley wants 7 coins for her dollar. _____

3. Tristan wants 19 coins for his dollar. _____

4. Lauren wants 25 coins for her dollar. _____

5. Callie wants 16 coins for her dollar. _____

6. Ty wants 6 coins for his dollar. _____

7. Andrew wants 10 coins for his dollar. _____

8. Ellen wants 1 coin for her dollar. _____

9. Chelsea wants 17 coins for her dollar. _____

10. Michael wants 28 coins for his dollar. _____

Now draw the coins you could use for the following dollar amounts.

| $1.45 | $2.44 | $1.76 |
|-------|-------|-------|
| $1.01 | $2.55 | $1.81 |

42

# Add or Subtract

Place + and − signs between the digits so that both sides of each equation are equal. The first one has been done for you.

1.   2   +   4   +   2   +   2   −   3   =   7

2.   9    9    9    2    2   =   9

3.   5    5    5    4    3   =   8

4.   1    2    3    4    5   =   9

5.   7    6    2    3    8   =   16

6.   5    3    2    4    1   =   9

7.   5    1    1    3    4   =   14

8.   8    1    6    2    8   =   11

9.   2    1    8    9    3   =   17

10.   7    6    5    4    3   =   9

11.   6    5    2    1    2   =   8

# Word Boxes

Each grid spells three words. Each word is written both horizontally and vertically. Fill in the missing spaces in the grid with a letter. Can you find the three words for each grid using the clues given? The first one has been done for you.

1.

|   | 1 | 2 | 3 |
|---|---|---|---|
| 1 | P | E | A |
| 2 | E | E | L |
| 3 | A | L | E |

1. green in a pod

2. electric snake

3. carbonated ginger

2.

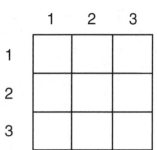

1. small, black insect

2. not, neither

3. to attempt

3.

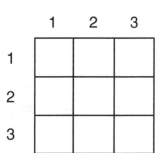

1. used to catch fish

2. bird like an ostrich

3. mummified Egyptian king

4.

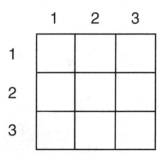

1. feline

2. how old a person is

3. number after nine

44

# Word Boxes *(cont.)*

See page 44 for the directions and an example.

5.

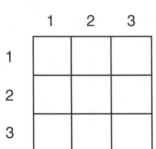

1. gives directions

2. time in the past

3. pan

6.

|   | 1 | 2 | 3 |
|---|---|---|---|
| 1 |   |   |   |
| 2 |   |   |   |
| 3 |   |   |   |

1. in addition, conjunction

2. another word for *no*

3. to change color

7.

|   | 1 | 2 | 3 |
|---|---|---|---|
| 1 |   |   |   |
| 2 |   |   |   |
| 3 |   |   |   |

1. to posses something

2. flatter, entice

3. head movement up and down

8.

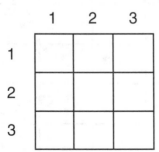

1. lightly touch pencil to table

2. you breathe it

3. to get open

# Logic Puzzles

Use the grid to help you solve each logic puzzle. Each letter fits on the grid with a corresponding number. Use the number sentences to help find the number that each letter represents. Put a star in the correct box on the grid that represents the letter. Put an "X" in each incorrect box.

1.

A + E = C

B + G = D

C + E = D

B + F = A

Hint: A = 5

|   | 1 | 2 | 3 | 4 | 5 | 6 | 7 |
|---|---|---|---|---|---|---|---|
| A |   |   |   |   | ☆ |   |   |
| B |   |   |   |   |   |   |   |
| C |   |   |   |   |   |   |   |
| D |   |   |   |   |   |   |   |
| E |   |   |   |   |   |   |   |
| F |   |   |   |   |   |   |   |
| G |   |   |   |   |   |   |   |

2. Create your own puzzle. Be sure to give a hint.

Number
Sentences:

|   | 1 | 2 | 3 | 4 | 5 | 6 | 7 |
|---|---|---|---|---|---|---|---|
| A |   |   |   |   |   |   |   |
| B |   |   |   |   |   |   |   |
| C |   |   |   |   |   |   |   |
| D |   |   |   |   |   |   |   |
| E |   |   |   |   |   |   |   |
| F |   |   |   |   |   |   |   |
| G |   |   |   |   |   |   |   |

# Many Multiples

The two rectangles show multiples of two different numbers. The common multiples are missing. All the numbers are less than 50. The center section, where the two rectangles intersect, is left blank. This is where the common multiples should go.

1. What are the two numbers being compared?

   _____

2. What are the common multiples? Write them in the center section as well.

   _____

3. How do you know?

   _____

   _____

   _____

   _____

| | |
|---|---|
| 35 | 30 |
| 5 | 10 |
| 45 | |
| 15 | 25 |

| | | | |
|---|---|---|---|
| 4 | 32 | 8 | 36 |
| 24 | 28 | 16 | |
| 48 | 44 | 12 | |

4. Now create a math puzzle using any of the multiples from the above problem. Share your puzzle with another student.

# Initial Equations

Each equation below contains the first letters of words that will make it complete. Find the missing words. An example has been done for you.

| 4 = Q in a G | 4 quarts in a gallon |
|---|---|

1. 366 = D in a LY _____

2. 6 = S of a H _____

3. 13 = T in a BD _____

4. 4 = Q in a D _____

5. 9 = P on a BT _____

6. 3 = t in a T _____

7. 64 = S on a CB _____

8. 16 = O in a P _____

9. 52 = C in a D _____

10. 26 = V in your S _____

11. 88 = K on a P _____

12. 8 = P in the SS _____

13. 5 = L in the GL _____

48

# Mixed-Up Riddles

Can you solve the riddles? Think before you write.

1. As soon as it's spoken, it's broken. What is it?

2. What runs up and down the stairs without moving?

3. What gets wetter and wetter the more it dries?

4. I'm lighter than a feather and yet the strongest person has trouble holding me for more than a minute. What am I?

5. I move and jump, copying your exact movements, but I never see you. What am I?

6. In me, *yesterday* follows *today*, and *tomorrow* is somewhere in between. What am I?

7. I'm locked up tight. The only way to get me out is by breaking me. What am I?

8. I can be seen, but I weigh nothing. Put me in a bucket or pail and I will make it a lighter load. What am I?

9. What runs, but can't walk? What has a mouth, but never talks? What has a bed, but never goes to sleep?

10. I can be thrown off a tall building and I won't break. I can be thrown into a car, and still I won't break. But, if you throw me in a river or the ocean, I will slowly break into pieces. What am I?

# Parts of a Word

The letters below are chunks or parts of words that have been removed. They belong somewhere in the middle of a word. Think of one or more words that contain these letters (in the same order) in it. An example has been done for you.

---

osoe = wh<u>osoe</u>ver

---

1. rehen

   _____

2. mbre

   _____

3. aar

   _____

4. drob

   _____

5. uee

   _____

6. ofre

   _____

7. ttre

   _____

8. mert

   _____

9. ncho

   _____

10. laim

    _____

# Rearrange It!

Rearrange the letters in each word to create a word. Once each word has been unscrambled, take the first letter of each of these words and unscramble them to determine the final word.

---

## Puzzle #1

Step 1: Unscramble each word.

1. ettoar     _____

2. nvpeleoe     _____

3. cefa     _____

4. srswcoodr     _____

5. peno     _____

Step 2: Now take the first letter of each word and unscramble them to form a new word. One letter has been placed for you.

_____ o _____ _____ _____

---

## Puzzle #2

Step 1: Unscramble each word.

1. aleimnr     _____

2. ctceielr     _____

3. alegn     _____

4. tresrgie     _____

5. osterf     _____

Step 2: Now take the first letter of each word and unscramble them to form a new word. One letter has been placed for you.

f _____ _____ _____ _____

---

## Puzzle #3

Step 1: Unscramble each word.

1. reapocm     _____

2. ttiucnsr     _____

3. ksane     _____

4. htigl     _____

5. ezgraoni     _____

Step 2: Now take the first letter of each word and unscramble them to form a new word. One letter has been placed for you.

_____ _____ i _____ _____

---

# Input/Output

Find the rule for each input/output function and fill in the missing spaces. The first one has been done for you.

1.

| Input | 3 | 5 | 9 | 18 | 20 |
|---|---|---|---|---|---|
| Output | 6 | 8 | 12 | 21 | 23 |
| The rule: | Add three | | | | |

2.

| Input | 4 | | 8 | 10 | 12 |
|---|---|---|---|---|---|
| Output | 6 | | 10 | | 14 |
| The rule: | | | | | |

3.

| Input | 3 | 6 | 9 | 12 | 15 |
|---|---|---|---|---|---|
| Output | 0 | 3 | | | |
| The rule | | | | | |

4.

| Input | 5 | | 15 | 20 | 30 |
|---|---|---|---|---|---|
| Output | 10 | 20 | | | |
| The rule: | | | | | |

5.

| Input | 7 | 8 | | 10 | 11 |
|---|---|---|---|---|---|
| Output | 28 | 32 | | 40 | |
| The rule: | | | | | |

6.

| Input | 16 | 18 | 20 | 22 | 24 |
|---|---|---|---|---|---|
| Output | 8 | | | | 12 |
| The rule | | | | | |

52

# Coin Possibilities

Rachel received 27 cents in change after purchasing a pet gerbil. How many different combinations of coins could she have received from the store clerk? Make a list of all the possibilities. Use the space below to write all of the possibilities. One has been done for you.

**Hint:** There are 13 possibilities.

| Quarters | Dimes | Nickels | Pennies |
|----------|-------|---------|---------|
| 1 | | | 2 |
| | | | |
| | | | |
| | | | |
| | | | |
| | | | |
| | | | |
| | | | |
| | | | |
| | | | |
| | | | |
| | | | |

# Follow the Leader

Can you find the pattern for each sequence below?  Finish the sequence by filling in the spaces.

1.   /      /      ✷      ✷      /      /      ☐ ☐ ☐

2.   2      4      7      11      16      22      ☐ ☐ ☐

3.   A      A      B      C      C      D      ☐ ☐ ☐

4.   ☆      ♡      ♡      ☆      ♡      ♡      ☐ ☐ ☐

5.   +      –      X      +      –      X      ☐ ☐ ☐

6.   △      ○      △      ○      ○      △      ☐ ☐ ☐

7.   1      3      1      4      1      5      ☐ ☐ ☐

8.   &      0      &      )      &      0      ☐ ☐ ☐

9.   G      G      A      G      G      A      ☐ ☐ ☐

10.   .6      .8      .10      .12      .14      .16      ☐ ☐ ☐

54

# Fill in the Blanks

There are 9 blank squares in each row of four number sentences. Use the digits 1 through 9 to complete these number sentences. You may use each digit only once and you must use all of the digits. The given numbers (not in boxes) do not count as part of the needed digits from 1 to 9. Two hints are given in the first row. These numbers **do** count as part of the needed digits.

**A.**

☐ x 3 = ③    ☐ − ☐ / 1    ☐ ÷ 4 = ☐    ☐ + ☐ / ⑨

**B.**

☐ + ☐ = 10    ☐ − ☐ / 5    ☐ ÷ ☐ = ☐    16 − ☐ / ☐

**C.**

☐ + ☐ = 13    ☐ − ☐ / 3    18 ÷ ☐ = ☐    ☐ + ☐ + ☐ / 8

**D.**

☐ + ☐ = 10    ☐ x ☐ / 15    ☐ x ☐ = 56    ☐ − ☐ + ☐ / 8

# School Bus Crossing

The school bus from Greenville Elementary School makes six stops each afternoon. Use the clues to determine the order in which the bus stops. The bus stops at the closest house first, then the second closest, and so forth until it gets to the house that is furthest from the school.

**Clues**

1. Melissa is the last stop.

2. Derek's stop is immediately after Laura.

3. Greg lives farther from school than Hannah, but not as far as Derek.

4. Hannah lives closer to the school than Mike.

5. Laura lives closer to the school than Melissa.

6. Laura lives closer to the school than Mike, but further than Greg.

Use the space below to draw a picture to help solve the problem.

# A Broken Keyboard

The keyboard of a computer was broken when this page was typed. Listed below are familiar phrases, but they are missing some important letters. All of the vowels have been replaced with x's. Discover what each phrase says and write it correctly on the line. The first one has been done for you.

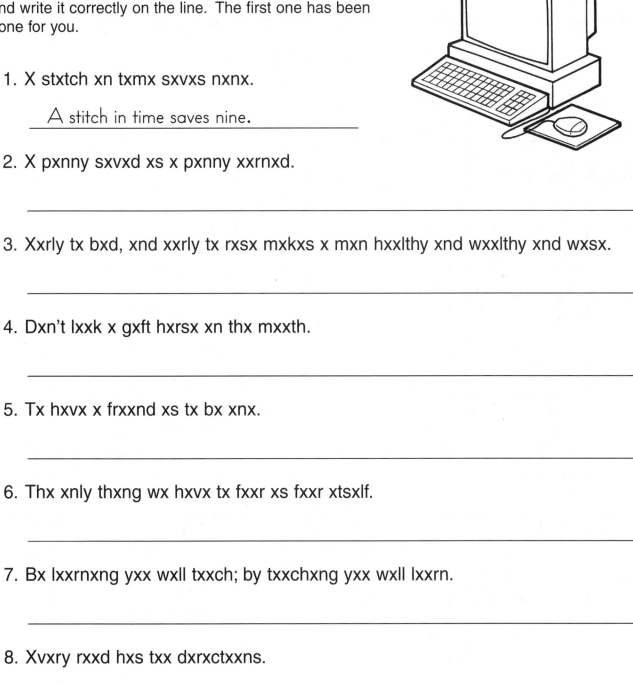

1. X stxtch xn txmx sxvxs nxnx.

   _A stitch in time saves nine._

2. X pxnny sxvxd xs x pxnny xxrnxd.

   _____

3. Xxrly tx bxd, xnd xxrly tx rxsx mxkxs x mxn hxxlthy xnd wxxlthy xnd wxsx.

   _____

4. Dxn't lxxk x gxft hxrsx xn thx mxxth.

   _____

5. Tx hxvx x frxxnd xs tx bx xnx.

   _____

6. Thx xnly thxng wx hxvx tx fxxr xs fxxr xtsxlf.

   _____

7. Bx lxxrnxng yxx wxll txxch; by txxchxng yxx wxll lxxrn.

   _____

8. Xvxry rxxd hxs txx dxrxctxxns.

   _____

# Boggle the Mind

Look at the letters in the grids below. How many words can you think of using the given letters? Follow the rules below to find the answer.

**Rules:**

*You must use the central letter of the grid as the beginning letter of each word.

*No letter can be used more than the number of times it is given.

*Letters do not need to be connected.

*No proper nouns or slang words allowed.

Two examples of words are given for the first grid.

1.

| L | O | D |
|---|---|---|
| B | **F** | N |
| I | L | D |

<u>Words</u>
fib
fill

2.

| M | T | A |
|---|---|---|
| I | **L** | N |
| D | E | F |

<u>Words</u>

3.

| L | A | B |
|---|---|---|
| I | **C** | R |
| L | S | T |

<u>Words</u>

# Boggle the Mind *(cont.)*

See page 58 for the directions and rules.

4.

| X | L | I |
|---|---|---|
| A | **T** | P |
| M | B | E |

Words

5.

| D | N | A |
|---|---|---|
| U | **B** | S |
| T | F | L |

Words

6.

| R | T | A |
|---|---|---|
| P | **S** | D |
| U | O | N |

Words

# Analogies

To complete an analogy, you must first determine the relationship between the given items. The relationship might be a person or thing to a place, position, location, or size. They are read as follows:

> The Great Depression : 1930s :: World War II : 1940s
>
> (The Great Depression is to the 1930s as World War II is to the 1940s)

1. first: George Washington::current: _____

2. northernmost U.S. city: Barrow, AK:: southernmost U.S. city: _____

3. Phoenix: Arizona:: Providence: _____

4. Democrat: Bill Clinton:: Republican: _____

5. Rosalynn Carter: Jimmy Carter:: Jacqueline Kennedy: _____

6. lake: ocean:: stream: _____

7. morning: breakfast:: night: _____

8. braces: teeth:: contact lenses: _____

9. sing: song:: read: _____

10. fingers: hand:: toes: _____

11. frame: picture:: curtain rod: _____

12. author: story:: poet: _____

13. hard: soft:: big: _____

14. Lincoln: Abraham:: Roosevelt: _____

15. tennis: racket:: baseball: _____

16. nephew: aunt:: niece: _____

17. wide: narrow:: long: _____

18. scissors: cut:: pen: _____

# Double or Nothing

Use the following clues to find words that contain consecutive double letters. An example has been done for you.

1. an animal _____ kangar**oo** _____

2. one of the four seasons _____

3. ants in your pants _____

4. paper used in secret voting _____

5. poem of fourteen lines _____

6. full of grief, very sad _____

7. two lines running side by side _____

8. paired with salt _____

9. famous pirate _____

10. winged insect _____

11. man on the . . . _____

12. silly drawing _____

13. sport played with helmets on _____

14. a poor person needing food _____

15. a flock of geese _____

16. similar to a crocodile _____

17. something has been loaned to you _____

18. classical dance _____

19. pieces of a . . . _____

20. use your brain, or a pasta _____

# Hidden Meanings #1

Explain the hidden meaning of each box.

|  |  |  |
|---|---|---|
| W<br>A<br>T<br>E<br>R | vitamins<br>vitamins<br>vitamins<br>vitamins<br>vitamins | vision vision |

1. _____  2. _____  3. _____

|  |  |  |
|---|---|---|
| le        g | $\dfrac{\text{vacation}}{\text{ccccc}}$ | sssssssssse |

4. _____  5. _____  6. _____

|  |  |  |
|---|---|---|
| CH**MADE**INA | ha  rm  on  y | SDRAW |

7. _____  8. _____  9. _____

|  |  |  |
|---|---|---|
| KCAB KCAB | BDSPELER | chimney<br>chimney<br>chimney<br>chimney<br>chimney |

10. _____  11. _____  12. _____

# Hidden Meanings #2

Explain the hidden meaning of each box.

E     E
Y  Y
E
D  D

mce
mce
mce

s      s
t      r
a     i
i     a
r     t
s     s

1. _____

2. _____

3. _____

poFISHnd

$$\frac{mind}{matter}$$

str**stars**ipes

4. _____

5. _____

6. _____

skating
thin ice

☆ ☆ ☆
beneath

N
W
O
T

7. _____

8. _____

9. _____

you JUST me

$$\frac{long}{due}$$

Loosen

10. _____

11. _____

12. _____

# The Five Senses

We each have five senses that help us live and learn in our environment. Take a minute to think how you used your five senses today.

What did you see today?  List at least 15 things.

_____

_____

_____

_____

What did you hear today?  List at least 15 things.

_____

_____

_____

_____

What did you touch/feel today?  List at least 15 things.

_____

_____

_____

_____

What did you smell today?  List at least five things.

_____

_____

_____

_____

What did you taste today?  List at least five things.

_____

_____

_____

_____

# You've Been Clipped

Write at least fifteen things you can do with a paper clip.  Be creative.  Go beyond the normal expectations for a paper clip.

1. _____

2. _____

3. _____

4. _____

5. _____

6. _____

7. _____

8. _____

9. _____

10. _____

11. _____

12. _____

13. _____

14. _____

15. _____

# Reduce, Recycle, Reuse

What could you do with. . .

Ball point pens that have run out of ink?

_____

_____

_____

_____

_____

Paint cans that are empty?

_____

_____

_____

_____

_____

Fruits or vegetables that have gone bad?

_____

_____

_____

_____

_____

# Time Capsule

Make a prediction about how the following items will change in the future. Think creatively. You may just create a new concept!

What will schools be like in the future?  Who will teach?  What will be taught?

_____

_____

_____

_____

_____

What will the United States be like in 50 years?  Will we be at war?

_____

_____

_____

_____

_____

How will music be different 100 years from now?  On what will music be played?

_____

_____

_____

_____

_____

What will clothes be like in 100 years?  What will be the styles?

_____

_____

_____

_____

_____

# Not a Chance!

Name four things you probably will never see.

1. _____   3. _____

2. _____   4. _____

Name four things you probably will never hear.

1. _____   3. _____

2. _____   4. _____

Name four things you cannot copy.

1. _____   3. _____

2. _____   4. _____

Name six people you probably will never meet.

1. _____   4. _____

2. _____   5. _____

3. _____   6. _____

Name two things that you think you are too old to do.

1. _____   2. _____

# Squiggle Drawing

Look at each squiggle shape in the boxes below. Finish the squiggle shape to create a real object. Write the name of the object on the line.

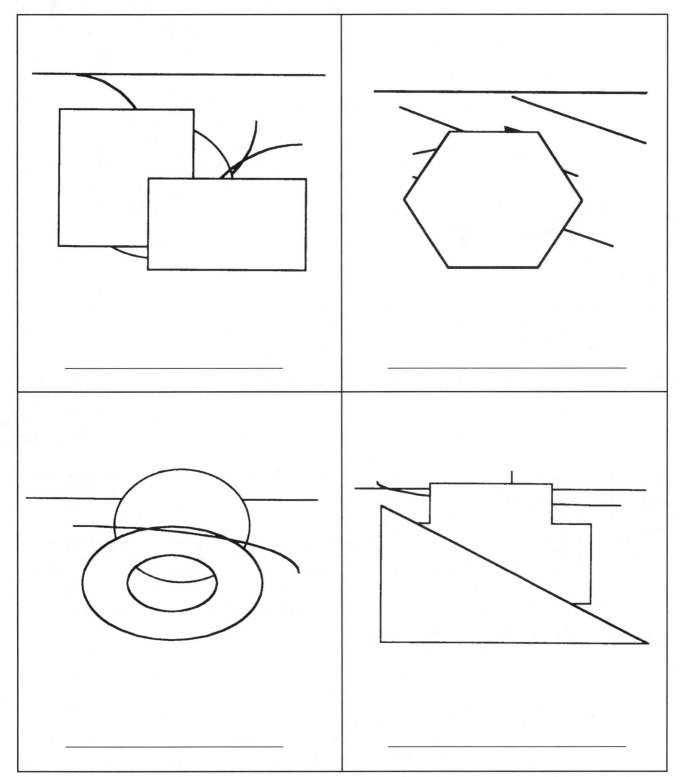

# Brainstorming Ideas

List objects that have a steering wheel.

_____

_____

_____

List 15 three-syllable words.  (Like *al-pha-bet*)

_____

_____

_____

List words associated with eating.

_____

_____

_____

List objects that have a handle.

_____

_____

_____

List at least ten adverbs.

_____

_____

_____

List your favorite things to do in the summer.

_____

_____

_____

70

# Formula for Success

In today's world, you need many skills in order to be successful. Answer the following questions to help you plan for success.

1. List the specific skills you need to be successful in today's world.

   _____

   _____

   _____

2. What things should you avoid in order to find success?

   _____

   _____

   _____

3. List five goals you have for the future.

   _____

   _____

   _____

   _____

4. How can you accomplish these goals?

   _____

   _____

   _____

5. What are typical stumbling blocks people experience that get in the way of goals and success?

   _____

   _____

   _____

6. How can these stumbling blocks be avoided or overcome?

   _____

   _____

   _____

# How Many?

1. eggs in a baker's dozen? _____

2. letters in the alphabet? _____

3. sides on an octagon? _____

4. days in a leap year? _____

5. cards in a standard deck? _____

6. weeks in a year? _____

7. centimeters in a decimeter? _____

8. feet in a yard? _____

9. degrees in a right angle? _____

10. keys on a piano? _____

11. squares on a checkerboard? _____

12. states in the United States? _____

13. years in a millennium? _____

14. planets in our solar system? _____

15. cups in a quart? _____

16. events in a triathlon? _____

17. continents are there? _____

18. miles in a marathon? _____

19. vertebrae in the spinal cord? _____

20. hours in a week? _____

# Imagine All the Learning

Imagine that you have been selected to make changes in the school curriculum. What would you change? Determine five changes that you would make. Explain your reasons for each change.

| **Change** | **Reason** |
|---|---|
| 1. _____ | _____ |
| | _____ |
| | _____ |
| 2. _____ | _____ |
| | _____ |
| | _____ |
| 3. _____ | _____ |
| | _____ |
| | _____ |
| 4. _____ | _____ |
| | _____ |
| | _____ |
| 5. _____ | _____ |
| | _____ |
| | _____ |

# Create a Fairy Tale

Create a new fairy tale to be shared through the ages. You must use all of the words from the castle towers in your fairy tale.

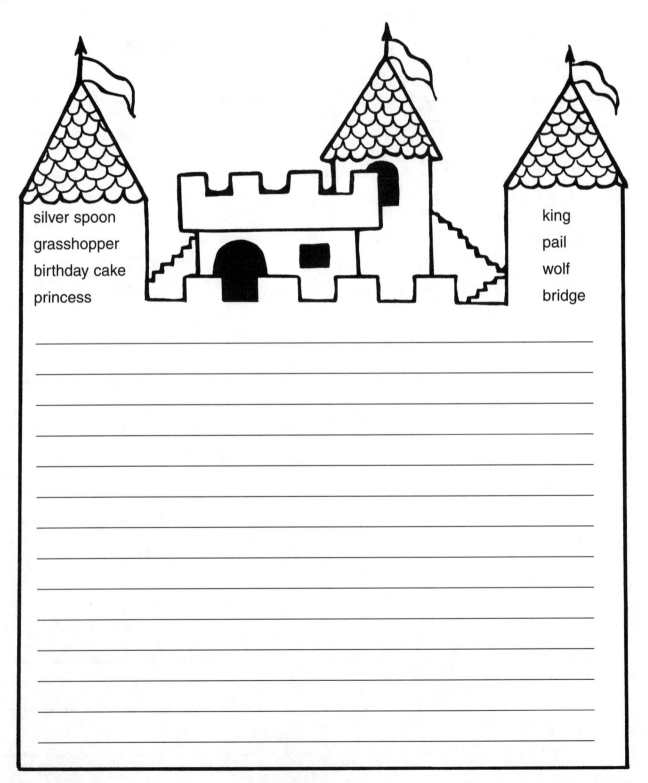

silver spoon
grasshopper
birthday cake
princess

king
pail
wolf
bridge

_____
_____
_____
_____
_____
_____
_____
_____
_____
_____
_____
_____
_____

# If You Could

Write what you would do if you were given the following opportunities:

1. If you could talk to a gorilla, what would you ask or say?

_____

_____

_____

2. If you could build your own ship, where would you sail? Why?

_____

_____

_____

3. If you could have a pet dolphin, what would you do with it?

_____

_____

_____

4. If you could own a store, what types of things would you sell? Why?

_____

_____

_____

5. If you could publish a book, what would it be about?

_____

_____

_____

# Push and Pull

Write as many things as you can think of for the following categories. Draw pictures, if necessary.

| What can you push? | What can you pull? |
|---|---|
|  |  |

| What can you jump? | What can you climb? | What can you race? |
|---|---|---|
|  |  |  |

| What can you ride? | What can you weigh? | What can you measure? |
|---|---|---|
|  |  |  |

# Categorize It

Arrange the words below into groups of your choice. Give each group a title or category. Use the white space to create the groups. Be prepared to explain your decisions on the lines provided below.

| | | | |
|---|---|---|---|
| cinnamon | fence | envelope | children |
| television | fifteen | grapes | croissants |
| star | object | open | pens |
| armoire | pencils | rice | happily |

_____

_____

_____

_____

_____

# A Hero

We hear about heroes every day. What is a hero? Describe your idea of a hero below.

What is your definition of a hero? _____

_____

_____

_____

What are the common characteristics of a hero? _____

_____

_____

_____

List some examples of heroes you know. _____

_____

_____

_____

What are some heroic acts? _____

_____

_____

_____

Can you identify some commonly known heroes? _____

_____

_____

_____

_____

# Ten Questions

Write a question for each of the following answers.

1. **Question:** _____

   Answer: The equator.

2. **Question:** _____

   Answer: They are gems and minerals.

3. **Question:** _____

   Answer: A blade of grass.

4. **Question:** _____

   Answer: It means the same thing as a trail.

5. **Question:** _____

   Answer: They are examples of odd numbers.

6. **Question:** _____

   Answer: These are the four types of sentences.

7. **Question:** _____

   Answer: The President of the United States.

8. **Question:** _____

   Answer: There were thirteen.

9. **Question:** _____

   Answer: April 15th of every year.

10. **Question:** _____

    Answer: It is a cupboard.

# In Common

What do the two items in each group have in common?

| | |
|---|---|
| peach and pear | potato and carrot |
| somersault and monkey bars | wheel and handle |
| shoe and umbrella | chalk and clipboard |
| cardboard and tree | lasagna and enchiladas |
| rake and broom | car and sled |

# What Do You Think?

Categorize the words in the box into six categories.  Place each word under the correct category.  For example, *jump* belongs in the "Verb" category.  Four words belong under each category.

| | | | |
|---|---|---|---|
| ~~jump~~ | book | they | opened |
| he | found | gorgeous | loudly |
| thick | green | so | glasses |
| forcefully | happily | and | but |
| it | flew | George Washington | yet |
| heavy | she | sleepily | mother |

| Noun | Verb | Pronoun |
|---|---|---|
| _____ | jump | _____ |
| _____ | _____ | _____ |
| _____ | _____ | _____ |
| _____ | _____ | _____ |

| Conjunction | Adverb | Adjective |
|---|---|---|
| _____ | _____ | _____ |
| _____ | _____ | _____ |
| _____ | _____ | _____ |
| _____ | _____ | _____ |

Can you write a sentence using one word from each category?_____

_____

_____

# Famous Americans

The names of 15 famous Americans have been split into two-letter or three-letter segments. The letters of the segments are in order, but the segments are scrambled. Put the pieces together to identify the famous American. The first one has been done for you.

1. UM AN HA TR RRY             Harry Truman
_____

2. SA PA RO RKS
_____

3. GE SH OR IN ON GE WA GT
_____

4. HN GL JO EN
_____

5. LD RA RD GE FO
_____

6. KE HE LEN LL ER
_____

7. FK NE JO EN DY HN
_____

8. NG MA JR RT LU IN TH ER KI
_____

9. RA YS NT UL SE SG
_____

10. SN LT DI EY WA
_____

11. MS JO ADA HN
_____

12. IN KL BE IN NJ FR AM AN
_____

13. TU HA BM RR AN IET
_____

14. LL IN TON CL BI
_____

15. FO HE RD NRY
_____

     82     

# Set the Clock

Think of as many words as you can for each category below. Give yourself three minutes for each. How many words will you think of?

A Circus

The Solar System

The Police Station

Ice Cream

Plant Life

# They Come in Pairs

Set your timer for five minutes and list as many things as you can think of that come in pairs. Can you think of at least twenty?

1. _____

2. _____

3. _____

4. _____

5. _____

6. _____

7. _____

8. _____

9. _____

10. _____

11. _____

12. _____

13. _____

14. _____

15. _____

16. _____

17. _____

18. _____

19. _____

20. _____

# It's in the Answer

Use one or more of the letters of the alphabet to answer each of the clues. The first one has been done for you.

1. not difficult                                      EZ _____

2. girl's name _____

3. sleep _____

4. vegetable _____

5. question _____

6. something to drink _____

7. insect _____

8. plant or vine _____

9. body of water _____

10. exclamation _____

11. goodbye _____

12. cold _____

13. pronoun _____

14. toilet paper _____

15. radio announcer _____

16. small bullet _____

17. to see with _____

18. a loan _____

# Related

Circle the word on the right that matches or is related in some way to the word in bold on the left.

| | | | | |
|---|---|---|---|---|
| 1. | **Language Arts** | writing | song | P.E. |
| 2. | **mammal** | snake | lizard | whale |
| 3. | **Senate** | 2 districts | 4 representatives | 6 years |
| 4. | **Supreme Court** | Judicial | Executive | Legislative |
| 5. | **primary color** | purple | green | yellow |
| 6. | **addition** | subtract | sum | multiple |
| 7. | **appeal** | orange | course | court |
| 8. | **handshake** | baby | introduction | study |
| 9. | **suffrage** | suffering | vote | tyranny |
| 10. | **auditory** | eyes | ears | nose |
| 11. | **South America** | Brazil | Russia | Anchorage |
| 12. | **tallest building** | Statue of Liberty | Capitol Building | Sears Tower |
| 13. | **milk** | sunglasses | moustache | blouse |

# Making Connections

Write as many sentences as you can using all of the following words:

| day | lollipop | critical | lead | tickled | shoe |
|---|---|---|---|---|---|

1. _____

_____

2. _____

_____

3. _____

_____

4. _____

_____

5. _____

_____

6. _____

_____

7. _____

_____

8. _____

_____

9. _____

_____

10. _____

_____

# Answer Key

## Page 4, From Beginning to End

add, aid, lid, lit, nit, nut, net, new, now, tow, too, zoo

## Page 5, Know Your ABCs

1. acrobat
2. alliance
3. alligator
4. ambulance
5. ancient
6. angrily
7. axle
8. backwards
9. captain
10. credible
11. emotions
12. envy
13. errand
14. eviction
15. forcible

## Page 6, License Plate Limbo

1. I'm hot
2. burn rubber
3. I go for it
4. Your plate here
5. black velvet
6. ladybug
7. lovin' you
8. our secret
9. a U2 fan
10. antique lover
11. for an angel or foreign angel
12. basketball star or baseball star
13. PT Cruiser
14. I'm too busy
15. You are nosy
16. Rescue 911

## Page 7, Salt and Pepper

1. sugar
2. black
3. dollars
4. prim
5. pencil
6. trip, stumble, summer, spring, winter, rise
7. big
8. black
9. in
10. up
11. sticks
12. thick
13. tall, long
14. cats
15. back
16. peace
17. cream
18. hammer, tooth
19. cheese
20. bacon/ham

## Page 8, What's in the Fridge?

Answers will vary.

## Page 9, What's a Palindrome?

1. ewe
2. Bob
3. tot
4. noon
5. wow
6. mum
7. Eve
8. gag
9. peep
10. bib
11. radar
12. solos
13. SOS
14. dad, pop
15. pop

# Answer Key (cont.)

16. racecar
17. Hannah
18. deed

## Page 10, Decode the Code

Imagine Yourself Succeeding!

## Page 11, That's an Oxymoron!

tight slacks

deafening silence

jumbo shrimp

living dead

healthy tan

mournful optimist

peace force

pretty ugly

same difference

silent scream

taped live

work party

## Page 12, Testing the Experiment

Answers will vary. Here are some possibilities:

Four-letter words: pear, tent, note, reap, rent, tame, meat, part, tape, time, team, tear, tore, torn, apex, nine, neon, trim, trip

Five-letter words: meant, extra, tempt, prime

Six-letter words: expert, nation, ration, permit

Seven-letter words: mention, primate, termite

Eight or more letter words: experiment, permanent, partition, penitent, pertinent

## Page 13–14, What's in Box #1?

Clue 1: egg, Clue 2: peck, Clue 3: scratch, Clue 4: lay, Clue 5: feather

Answer: Chicken

## Page 15–16, What's in Box #2?

Clue 1: run, Clue 2: kick, Clue 3: forward, Clue 4: field, Clue 5: goalie

Answer: Soccer or Soccer Ball

## Page 17, The Letter *E*

1. execute
2. eagle
3. exhale
4. envelope
5. escape
6. encourage
7. estimate
8. entice
9. ewe
10. evacuate
11. able
12. airplane
13. ape
14. angle
15. altitude
16. apple
17. abuse
18. antique

## Page 18, Which Is the Imposter?

1. Bartlett

   Bartlett is a pear; the rest are apples.

2. nephew

   A *nephew* is a male; the rest are female titles.

3. August

   August is the only month in which we don't celebrate a holiday.

4. Calculus

   Calculus is a math subject; the rest are clouds.

5. Oxygen

   Oxygen is a gas; the rest are shapes.

6. Ounce

   Ounce is not part of the Metric system.

7. Orange

   Orange is not a primary color.

8. Sum

   *Sum* is a word related to addition; the others are related to multiplication.

9. Dogwood

   Dogwood is a tree; the rest are flowers.

# Answer Key *(cont.)*

10. Turtle

    The turtle is the only animal on the list that does not jump or hop.

## Page 19, Question of the Day
Answers will vary.

## Page 20, The Long and Short of It
1. mathematics
2. physical education
3. referee
4. champion
5. television
6. limousine
7. doctor
8. examination
9. telephone
10. refrigerator
11. airplane
12. president

13–17. Answers will vary.

## Page 21, You're a Funny Bunny
2. cat mat
3. horse course
4. roast toast
5. grape ape
6. bug hug
7. care bear
8. pooch smooch
9. lazy daisy
10. big pig
11. rude dude
12. fat cat
13. sad lad
14. tan fan
15. sad dad
16. bug rug
17. mellow fellow
18. spare mare
19. mouse house
20. slick chick

## Page 22, Cut It Short
1. As soon as possible
2. Etcetera
3. New York City
4. United States of America
5. National Aeronautics Administration
6. National Basketball Association
7. District Attorney
8. I owe you
9. railroad
10. doctor
11. Federal Bureau of Investigation
12. Internal Revenue Service
13. Before Christ
14. Drug Abuse Resistance Education
15. Cash on Delivery
16. National Football League
17. post script
18. Vermont
19. April
20. Emergency Medical Technician

## Page 23, Word Chains
Answers will vary.

## Page 24, Super Solutions
1. mode = 30
2. 11:10 A.M.
3. 45
4. $2.45
5. May 6
6. 37 laps

## Page 25, Athletically Inclined
Anne – volleyball

Elise – basketball

Ethan – swimming

Katie – baseball

Logan – soccer

Kevin – track

# Answer Key *(cont.)*

## Page 26, Money Matters

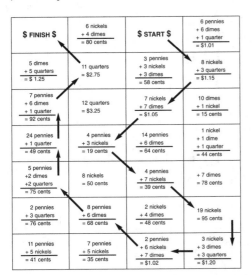

## Page 27, Sequencing Squares

64, 256

You multiply by four each time. 4 x 4 = 16,
16 x 4 = 64, 64 x 4 = 256

## Page 28, Question Quiz

Answers will vary. Here are some possibilities:

Question: Maren counted 12 red, 6 orange, and
6 yellow butterflies. How many did she count
all together?

Question: Mrs. Jones has twenty-four students
in her class. She needs to divide them into four
groups. How many students will be in each
group?

Question: The Cardiff family received five free
passes to the skating rink. There are three girls
and two boys in the family. How many free
passes will each child receive?

## Page 29, My Favorite Day

Answers will vary.

## Page 30, Geometrically Speaking

A – 6 – red

B – 2 – white

C – 8 – orange

D – 3 – green

E – 7 – blue

F – 5 – purple

## Page 31, *Calots* and *Wiggles*

A *calot* is a figure is divided symmetrically in
half using a vertical line.

A *wiggle* is a circular figure. Notice each shape
is always rounded on the outer edge.

## Page 32, Is It Symmetrical?

1. 1
2. 8
3. 4
4. 1
5. 2
6. 6

## Page 33, Number Sentences

Answers will vary.

## Page 34, Reckless Rearranging

10 + 9 + 1 = 20

16 + 2 + 2 = 20

12 + 4 + 4 = 20

3 + 6 + 11 = 20

8 + 5 + 7 = 20

The number 4 is left over.

## Page 35, Tricky Shapes

Triangles = 27

Quadrilaterals = 62

## Page 36, Final Grades

Paige – B

Peyton – A

Tanner – C-

Andrew – A+

Eve – D

Dwayne – C

## Page 37, What Comes Next?

64 x 4 = 256

64 x 5 = 320

24 x 4444 = 106,656

24 x 44444 = 1,066,656

6543 x 7 + 5 = 45,806

65432 x 7 + 4 = 458,028

Answers will vary.

# Answer Key *(cont.)*

**Page 38, Figure It Out!**

Andy Smith has a cat.

Bob King has a rabbit.

Allison Furth has a snake.

**Page 39, Solve the Puzzle**

E – 5 – yellow

F – 4 – blue

G – 8 – red

**Page 40, Triangulation**

Triangulation numbers are 3, 6, 10, and 21.

**Page 41, Stars and Stripes**

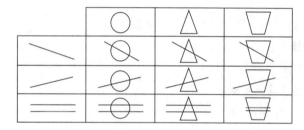

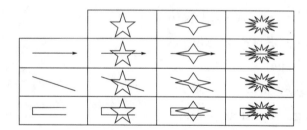

**Page 42, Keep the Change**

1. 5 dimes, 10 nickels

2. 2 quarters, 5 dimes

3. 9 dimes, 10 pennies

4. 1 quarter, 3 dimes, 6 nickels, 15 pennies

5. 2 quarters, 4 dimes, 10 pennies

6. 3 quarters, 2 dimes, 1 nickel

7. 10 dimes

8. 1 silver dollar

9. 7 dimes, 5 nickels, 5 pennies

10. 3 quarters, 25 pennies

Answers will vary.

**Page 43, Add or Subtract**

1. $2 + 4 + 2 + 2 - 3 = 7$

2. $9 - 9 + 9 - 2 + 2 = 9$ or $9 + 9 - 9 + 2 - 2 = 9$

3. $5 + 5 + 5 - 4 - 3 = 8$

4. $1 + 2 - 3 + 4 + 5 = 9$

5. $7 + 6 - 2 - 3 + 8 = 16$

6. $5 - 3 + 2 + 4 + 1 = 9$

7. $5 + 1 + 1 + 3 + 4 = 14$

8. $8 - 1 - 6 + 2 + 8 = 11$

9. $2 + 1 + 8 + 9 - 3 = 17$

10. $7 + 6 - 5 + 4 - 3 = 9$

11. $6 + 5 - 2 + 1 - 2 = 8$

**Page 44, Word Boxes**

1. pea, eel, ale

2. ant, nor, try

3. net, emu, tut

4. cat, age, ten

**Page 45, Word Boxes** *(cont.)*

5. map, ago, pot

6. and, nay, dye

7. own, woo, nod

8. tap, air, pry

**Page 46, Logic Puzzles**

1. A = 5

   B = 3

   C = 6

   D = 7

   E = 1

   F = 2

   G = 4

2. Answer will vary.

**Page 47, Many Multiples**

1. The two numbers being compared are 5 and 4.

2. The common multiples are 20 and 40.

3. You know because the multiples of 5 are in the top rectangle and the multiples of 4 are in the bottom rectangle.

4. Answers will vary.

# Answer Key *(cont.)*

**Page 48, Initial Equations**

1. 366 days in a leap year
2. 6 sides of a hexagon
3. 13 things in a baker's dozen
4. 4 quarters in a dollar
5. 9 players on a baseball team
6. 3 teaspoons in a tablespoon
7. 64 squares on a checkerboard
8. 16 ounces in a pound
9. 52 cards in a deck
10. 26 vertebrae in your spine
11. 88 keys on a piano
12. 8 planets in the solar system
13. 5 lakes in the Great Lakes

**Page 49, Mixed-Up Riddles**

1. a secret or silence
2. carpet/rug
3. a towel
4. your breath
5. a shadow
6. the dictionary
7. egg yolk
8. a hole
9. a river
10. a tissue

**Page 50, Parts of a Word**

Some possible answers are:

1. comprehend, comprehension, apprehend, reprehensible, incomprehensible
2. umbrella
3. aardvark, bazaar
4. wardrobe
5. queen, squeeze, squeegee
6. proofread, proofreader
7. mattress, buttress
8. summertime
9. anchor, anchored, poncho
10. claim, proclaim, exclaim

**Page 51, Rearrange It!**

Puzzle #1

1. rotate
2. envelope
3. face
4. crossword
5. open

FORCE

Puzzle #2

1. mineral
2. electric
3. angle
4. register
5. forest

FRAME

Puzzle #3

1. compare
2. instruct
3. snake
4. light
5. organize

COILS

**Page 52, Input/Output**

2. Input: 6
   Output: 8, 12
   Rule: Add input by two
3. Output: 6, 9, 12
   Rule: Subtract input by three
4. Input: 10
   Output: 30, 40, 60
   Rule: Multiply input by two
5. Input: 9
   Output: 36, 44
   Rule: Multiply input by four
6. Output: 9, 10, 11
   Rule: Divide input by two

# Answer Key *(cont.)*

## Page 53, Coin Possibilities

The 13 possibilities are:

1 quarter, 2 pennies

1 dime, 17 pennies

1 dime, 1 nickel, 12 pennies

1 dime, 2 nickels, 7 pennies

1 dime, 3 nickels, 2 pennies

2 dimes, 7 pennies

2 dimes, 1 nickel, 2 pennies

1 nickel, 22 pennies

2 nickels, 17 pennies

3 nickels, 12 pennies

4 nickels, 7 pennies

5 nickels, 2 pennies

27 pennies

## Page 54, Follow the Leader

1. ✶, ✶, /
2. 29, 37, 46
3. E, E, F
4. ☆ ♡ ♡
5. +, -, X
6. ◯, ◯, ◯
7. 1, 6, 1
8. &, ), &
9. G, G, A
10. .18, .20, .22

## Page 55, Fill in the Blanks

Answers will vary.

## Page 56, School Bus Crossing

After school, the bus stops at Hannah's, Greg's, Laura's, Derek's, Mike's, and then Melissa's house.

## Page 57, A Broken Keyboard

1. A stitch in time saves nine.
2. A penny saved is a penny earned.
3. Early to bed, and early to rise, makes a man healthy and wealthy and wise.
4. Don't look a gift horse in the mouth.
5. To have a friend is to be one.
6. The only thing we have to fear is fear itself.
7. By learning you will teach, by teaching you will learn.
8. Every road has two directions.

## Page 58, Boggle the Mind

Some possible answers are:

1. fib, fill, fin, find, foil, fond
2. left, lent, lend, lam, lit, lid, lad, life, lie, lime, let, lint, leaf, lean, lame, led, lane, late, land, lain, laid, lead, lift, line, lied
3. call, carts, calls, car, cart, cars, cast, cabs, cab, crab, crabs, cat, cats, crib, cribs

## Page 59, Boggle the Mind *(cont.)*

Some possible answers are:

4. tax, tab, tame, tape, tap, time, tip, tile, tale, tea, teal, team, tie, tail
5. bud, bun, but, buns, buds, bus, ban, bad, bat, bats, bald, blast, band, bands, bunt, ban, bans
6. son, sod, sop, sad, soar, sat, sun, sap, sand, sort, star, strap, sour, spur, spun, stop, snap, stud, span, stun, sort, stand, sport, sound, spud

## Page 60, Analogies

1. George W. Bush (or current president)
2. Hilo, Hawaii
3. Rhode Island
4. George W. Bush (or other prominent republican)
5. John F. Kennedy
6. river
7. dinner, supper
8. eyes
9. book
10. foot
11. window
12. poem
13. small, tiny, little
14. Theodore or Franklin

# Answer Key *(cont.)*

15. bat
16. uncle
17. short
18. write

## Page 61, Double or Nothing

1. kangaroo, alligator, aardvark, llama
2. summer, fall
3. wiggle
4. ballot
5. sonnet
6. depressed
7. parallel
8. pepper
9. Captain Hook
10. butterfly, bee
11. moon
12. doodle, scribble
13. football
14. beggar
15. gaggle
16. alligator
17. borrow
18. ballet
19. puzzle
20. noodle

## Page 62, Hidden Meanings #1

1. waterfall
2. multi-vitamins
3. double vision
4. broken leg
5. vacation overseas
6. Tennessee
7. Made in China
8. four-part harmony
9. backwards
10. double back
11. bad speller
12. chimney stack

## Page 63, Hidden Meanings #2

1. cross-eyed
2. three blind mice
3. upstairs, downstairs
4. big fish in a little pond
5. mind over matter
6. stars 'n stripes
7. skating on thin ice
8. beneath the stars
9. uptown
10. just between you and me
11. long over due
12. loosen up

## Pages 64–71

Answers will vary.

## Page 72, How Many?

1. 13
2. 26
3. 8
4. 366
5. 52
6. 52
7. 10
8. 3
9. 90
10. 88
11. 64
12. 50
13. 1,000
14. 9
15. 4
16. 3
17. 7
18. 26
19. 26
20. 168

# Answer Key *(cont.)*

**Pages 73 – 80**

Answers will vary.

**Page 81, What Do You Think?**

Noun:  book, George Washington, glasses, mother

Verb:  jump, flew, opened, found

Pronoun:  he, she, they, it

Conjunction:  but, yet, so, and

Adverb:  happily, sleepily, forcefully, loudly

Adjective:  thick, green, heavy, gorgeous

Sentences will vary.

**Page 82, Famous Americans**

1. Harry Truman
2. Rosa Parks
3. George Washington
4. John Glen
5. Gerald Ford
6. Helen Keller
7. John F. Kennedy
8. Martin Luther King, Jr.
9. Ulysses Grant
10. Walt Disney
11. John Adams
12. Benjamin Franklin
13. Harriet Tubman
14. Bill Clinton
15. Henry Ford

**Page 83–84**

Answers will vary.

**Page 85, It's in the Answer**

1. EZ
2. K, D, B
3. ZZZZ
4. P
5. Y
6. T
7. B
8. IV
9. C
10. O
11. CU
12. IC
13. I
14. TP
15. DJ
16. BB
17. I
18. IOU

**Page 86, Related**

1. writing
2. whale
3. 6 years
4. Judicial
5. yellow
6. sum
7. court
8. introduction
9. vote
10. ears
11. Brazil
12. Sears Tower
13. moustache

**Page 87, Making Connections**

Answers will vary.